Illiteracy

Look for these and other books in the Lucent Overview series:

Illiteracy

by Sean M. Grady

Library of Congress Cataloging-in-Publication Data

Grady, Sean M., 1965-
    Illiteracy / by Sean M. Grady
       p.   cm. — (Lucent overview series)
    Includes bibliographical references (p.   ) and index.
    Summary: Discusses the different forms or degrees of illiteracy
in the United States, how this problem affects people, and what is
being done about it.
    ISBN 1-56006-139-1 (alk. paper) :
    1. Literacy—United States—Juvenile literature.   2. Literacy
programs—Cross-cultural studies—Juvenile literature.
    [1. Literacy.]   I. Title.   II. Series.
LC151.G73   1994
302.2'244'0973—dc20

                                            93-19108
                                           CIP
                                           AC

Copyright © 1994 by Lucent Books, Inc.
P.O. Box 289011, San Diego, CA 92198-9011
Printed in the U.S.A.

Contents

Introduction

FOR MILLIONS OF people in the United States, the words in this book might well have been written in a secret code. To some of these people the words on this page are a meaningless string of letters. To others even the letters are unreadable, appearing as patterns of lines, squiggles, and other shapes. And more than just this book is a mystery—virtually every street sign, every newspaper advertisement, even every can label is a mass of unreadable information.

For tens of millions of other people in this country, these words would be less of a mystery. However, for these people reading is a mind-numbing chore, one in which they have to force their way through all but the shortest words. And while they can figure out what these words say, many of them would not be able to write down these ideas in their own words. For them, writing even a couple of clear, organized sentences is impossible.

These are just two of the forms of illiteracy that can be found throughout the United States today. The question of how to deal with illiteracy in all its forms has been an on again-off again issue for much of the twentieth century. In the late 1970s and early 1980s, the debate over illiteracy in the United States flared once again. Studies by various universities and private foundations claimed

(Opposite page) Schoolchildren learn a basic and important skill—how to read. Though a majority of Americans can read, as many as eighty million people may be illiterate to some degree.

7

that anywhere from thirty million to seventy-two million people had serious enough difficulty in reading and writing that they could be considered illiterate to some degree. These claims prompted a decade of studies and of calls for a major assault on illiteracy. The media carried advertisements and public service announcements promoting literacy. News stories focused on the daily struggles illiterate people face and the programs that exist to help them solve their problems. But aside from making more people aware of illiteracy, these drives had little effect. By 1992 literacy experts said that anywhere from thirty-five million to eighty million people suffered from some degree of illiteracy. Today, dealing with illiteracy remains an uncertain issue.

What is certain, though, is the effect illiteracy has on people. Contemporary America is a nation that functions largely through the use of the writ-

A man prepares a meal. A simple task like following a recipe can be difficult for a person unable to read.

ten word. Street signs, grocery coupons, apartment rental contracts, instruction manuals, newspapers, and a host of other everyday items are made with the assumption that people know how to read. People who cannot read and write are sometimes looked down on. As a result, some illiterate young people and adults spend their lives trying to cover up and work around their inability to read. They shop by memorizing shapes, colors, and pictures on labels. What is worse, every year students either give up on ever learning to read and drop out of school, or they graduate from high school (and sometimes from college) without having learned how to read and write.

Illiteracy begins in childhood, when some elementary school students start to fall behind their classmates. However, the major problems of illiteracy come about when illiterate students grow up. They find themselves in a world based on the written word, a world in which they have to make a life where they can both hide their illiteracy and work around it.

There are some signs that the nation is taking a long-term interest in fighting illiteracy. In 1991 President George Bush signed the National Literacy Act. This law promises to spend more than one billion dollars by 1995 to support national and local literacy organizations, as well as to set up a national literacy center for research into the problems of and proposed solutions for illiteracy. The sponsors of this law hope that it will allow literacy groups to exchange information and improve the quality of service they offer. However, the question of whether or not this new law will do a better job of breaking the chains of illiteracy than did similar measures in the past will not begin to be answered until the end of the twentieth century.

1

The Tragedy of Illiteracy

IN HIS 1980 book *Prisoners of Silence*, education activist Jonathan Kozol described how he discovered that a friend of his was illiterate. Kozol and his friend, a man named Peter, often went out for lunch or dinner together. Usually they ate at a national chain restaurant such as Denny's or Howard Johnson's. On one of these occasions, however, Kozol suggested they try a small seafood restaurant in a nearby town. Peter nervously agreed, but as they neared the restaurant, he pleaded with Kozol to go to a nearby Howard Johnson's instead. This they did.

As they ordered their meals, Kozol noticed something about his friend. Peter was using the pictures on the menu to order his meal. At that moment Kozol realized that Peter could not read. Like many other illiterate people Peter ate only at restaurants that had picture menus or where he could order something simple like a hamburger and a soda. Kozol also realized why his friend had pleaded with him to forego their trip to the unfamiliar seafood restaurant. The restaurant's pictureless written menu would have forced him to reveal his illiteracy, something he apparently could not bear to do.

(Opposite page) A shopper puzzles over the wide offering of medicines on a drugstore shelf. Her ability to read and comprehend product descriptions enables her to find the right medicine for her needs.

11

Millions of people in America today fight the same battles with illiteracy that Kozol's friend fought. They spend their lives trying to survive in a society that depends on the written word. Like Peter, they try to avoid having their friends or co-workers find out about their problems. They often are afraid that they will lose their jobs, their homes, and even their families if their illiteracy is discovered. And they think that people will look down on them because of their inability to read.

What is illiteracy?

Reading was not always the essential skill it is today. As recently as the turn of the century a person could get by fairly easily with minimal literacy skills. Even though the United States had become a great industrial power, there were many opportunities for success that did not require much reading or writing. Indeed, to be considered literate all a person had to do was write his or her own name. People in general had no pressing need for literacy in the modern sense—the ability to read and write at least as well as an eleventh- or twelfth-grade student. Some jobs required advanced levels of literacy, but many more did not.

Like many nineteenth- and early twentieth-century Americans, factory workers of the late 1800s could probably perform their jobs with minimal literacy skills.

Cigar factory workers of the 1920s. Though their jobs took skill and training, the work probably did not require the ability to read and write.

Most people—such as farmers, factory workers, seamstresses, and homemakers—could live, work, shop, and succeed in life without reading or writing at all.

As society and technology advanced, though, reading and writing became more important. People needed progressively greater literacy skills to keep up with the changing times. Workers had to be able to use the more complicated machinery that was being produced. Training for these machines required the ability to read large, detailed instruction manuals. And with the development and wide use of computers and computerized equipment, reading has become a standard skill for many jobs.

The demands of the modern workplace are a constant concern for underskilled and undereducated workers. Many of these workers have come to realize that their futures depend on upgrading various skills, including reading. Commenting about an Ohio assembly line worker, who would soon have to use computer-controlled robots, an adult education teacher said, "Years ago, that worker would have little to do with a literacy program. Now, he has enrolled in the program to keep his job."

A student learns about robotics. The high-technology, highly competitive modern workplace makes literacy a must.

A young woman checks the recipe before cooking. Modern daily life requires the ability to read and comprehend a variety of directions, recipes, and warnings.

Daily life, too, requires much more literacy than it once did. Printed documents, like newspapers, bus schedules, and instructions for a host of everyday items and appliances, provide people with essential information. Moreover, printed forms such as job applications or rental agreements demand that people read and then answer questions in writing. Those who cannot read basic materials such as these are more likely to become victims of their own inabilities. One Ohio newspaper recounted the story of a woman who had been driving for years without a license because she could not read well enough to pass the written test. The newspaper explained that she was involved in a car accident. Although the other driver was at fault, the woman would not make a police report or file an insurance claim because she feared she would be arrested for driving without a license.

Defining illiteracy

This story illustrates the difficulties faced by those who cannot read. Problems similar to this are a part of everyday life for millions of Americans. The most seriously illiterate people cannot read more than one or two simple words, like *bus* or *exit*. They cannot write or print their own names. Sometimes they cannot do simple arithmetic, like figuring change they are owed on a purchase. But the seriously illiterate make up only a small part of America's illiterate population. Literacy experts estimate their number at about five million, or roughly 2.5 percent of the nation's adult population.

The majority of America's illiterate adults have some literacy skills, though at widely different levels. Some may be able to read only at the level of an average third- or fourth-grade student. They might read or write short sentences using simple words but not be able to read instruction manuals or write business letters. Even short newspaper or magazine articles would be too advanced for them. Because their reading and writing skills are so poorly developed, these people are referred to as functionally illiterate.

The rest of the nation's illiterate adults actually can be called semi-literate or marginally literate. They can read and write at least as well as a typical sixth-grade student. They can understand simple newspaper stories and, with some effort, write short essays. Advanced, or adult-level, books are beyond them, as are many other documents.

Estimates of how many people are functionally illiterate and marginally literate vary widely. Some experts say that functionally illiterate adults number roughly thirty million, with marginally literate adults making up another twenty million. Together with adults who are totally illiterate, these groups would make up around 30 percent of America's adult population—nearly fifty-five million people. Other experts, though, say these figures are too low. *Illiterate America* author Jonathan Kozol once said that at least seventy-two million adults had some literacy problems. If this is true, then two out of every five adults can be classified as illiterate.

Experts agree that illiteracy can be found in all segments of society. Research suggests, however,

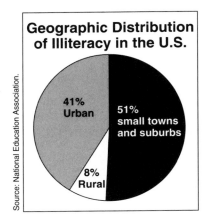

Geographic Distribution of Illiteracy in the U.S.

41% Urban

51% small towns and suburbs

8% Rural

Source: National Education Association.

that an illiterate person today probably is also poor and a high school dropout. Studies of poverty and illiteracy have shown that more than 40 percent of adults who live in poverty are at least functionally, if not totally, illiterate. Studies also show that, in terms of actual numbers, most illiterate Americans are white. But in relation to their numbers in the general population, a larger proportion of African Americans and Latinos are illiterate. Some studies suggest that more than 40 percent of all minority youths—including African Americans, Latinos, and native Americans—grow up without basic literacy skills.

A complex problem

The portrait of illiteracy that emerges from these studies suggests that illiteracy is a complex problem with many causes. While the educational system may be a part of the problem, many researchers believe illiteracy has its roots in the social ills that undermine many aspects of society.

The complexity of the problem of illiteracy was either unknown or ignored for decades. Instead, it was viewed as a simple personal affliction, sometimes stemming from a poor education, but mostly the result of laziness or other shortcomings. David Harman, in his 1987 book *Illiteracy: A National Dilemma*, said that this attitude still persists among many literate people, who "often assume that literacy is a natural condition and that the lack of literacy abilities is tantamount to being diseased."

But since the 1960s many literacy experts have pointed to studies of illiteracy, poverty, and racial discrimination to counter this mind-set. They say illiteracy is a social problem—an outgrowth of economic inequality and racial discrimination. "Illiterates are not 'afflicted'," Jonathan Kozol wrote in the late 1980s. "They are the products of an educational system that provides the children of the affluent with many times the yearly fiscal allocation [larger school budgets] granted to children of the poor."

But no matter what their background, people who cannot read or write share common concerns. Most feel a sense of shame about their lack of literacy skills and a fear of being found out. The story about Peter, the man who ate only at Howard Johnson's, is just one example of how illiterate people try to deal with their problem. A 1986 article from the *Atlanta Journal* describes how far people will go to hide their illiteracy:

> They are marvelous actors, capable of making themselves invisible, or at least unnoticeable, in a society that only occasionally realizes they exist. They may carry a newspaper wherever they go. Or show up with an arm in a sling on the day they have to fill out a form. Or maybe they just forgot their glasses. Many will quit their job rather than be unmasked.

John Corcoran, a land developer in California's San Diego County, was one such person. Like many people who grow up illiterate, he had been diagnosed as a slow student when he was young. Even so, his elementary school teachers had passed him on to higher grade levels. He used his charm and his popularity as a star basketball

Developer John Corcoran discusses construction plans with a client. Unable to read or write for many years, Corcoran faked his way through high school, college, and even his career. He was eventually forced to reveal his charade and overcome his disability.

player to convince his high school teachers to give him passing grades. And he used a number of techniques, which included getting fellow students to write term papers and take tests for him, to earn degrees from universities in Texas and California.

Deception

Corcoran was not a bad student. He understood his class lectures and could hold his own in group study sessions. However, he could not read his textbooks, write term papers, or take written tests. He tried to take classes that offered oral tests or take-homes that friends could do for him. Using these techniques he received his bachelor's degree and earned a master's degree in sociology two years later.

Corcoran decided to become a teacher, figuring his experience with his still-hidden disability would give him an edge in teaching other problem students. He established himself as an innovative history and social studies teacher at two San Diego County high schools. He was respected by principals and fellow teachers for his ability to get through to students with learning difficulties. He also, in the mid-1960s, set up a construction company with help from his brother-in-law. He hired secretaries, accountants, and lawyers to handle the company's paperwork. By 1979 Corcoran had retired from teaching, devoting himself to his construction business.

But Corcoran's illiteracy caught up with him. Real estate prices began to drop in the early 1980s. The houses Corcoran's company had built stopped selling; with no money coming in, he could not build houses on land he had bought to develop. In order to pay his bills, he began firing his office staff. Though he tried, he could not handle the company's paperwork himself. Investors withdrew their support; banks and other creditors began suing for the money he owed them. By 1986 John Corcoran saw his once-suc-

Now able to read and write, Corcoran helps other adults overcome their problems with reading and writing.

cessful company being buried by a mass of paperwork he could not comprehend.

He finally was able to turn his company around. But he knew that, without learning how to read and write, he would never be free of the threat of his business collapsing. He enrolled in a literacy training class at a local library, eventually learning to read and write well enough to run his business himself. Corcoran's announcement of his problems with illiteracy at a meeting of a county businesspeople's group went on to become national news. And he began lecturing on the importance of literacy and on the need for literacy classes for those, like himself, who had grown up illiterate.

A painful revelation

Corcoran's story is unusual. In all but a few cases illiterate people do not achieve this type of success. Nor are they able to learn to read and write as well as Corcoran did in as little time. But Corcoran's story dramatically illustrates how illiterate people—no matter what their standing in life—become skilled at covering up their problems and at finding ways to get through life. They do this even when it means deceiving themselves and others and living with the fear of discovery.

They do this not because they like living in a world without the written word but because revealing their problem can seem more painful than living with it. Society, some experts say, views illiteracy as a sign of stupidity rather than a problem that can be overcome. "The social stigma is much worse than [with] alcoholism or drug use," said Desiree Nickell, executive director of the Miami Valley Literacy Council in Ohio. "We have people speaking out nationally about a drinking problem or a drug problem, but illiteracy is something people don't want to talk about."

Qq Rr Ss Tt Uu Vv Ww
weren't
rich
wish
that
wouldn't
homeless
poor
food
lots
gold

2

The Causes of Illiteracy

LITERACY IS A skill, a technique of using patterns of letters to preserve ideas. The high value most societies place on the written word, however, sometimes masks the fact that literacy is not a natural phenomenon. Almost all people can *learn* how to read and write, but no one is born *knowing* how to read and write. To put it another way, every person is born illiterate.

Describing the causes of illiteracy, then, actually means explaining why some people stay illiterate. Studies of illiteracy in the 1970s and 1980s showed that there are many factors—educational, social, even physiological—that keep people from becoming literate. Rarely will any one factor stand alone. In most cases these factors combine to form a nearly impassable barrier across the path toward literacy.

Illiteracy and the schools

Public schools, as the primary educational institutions in this country, have a major role in developing literacy. Reading and writing are fundamental skills taught in all schools. But many students—up to one million each year—manage to complete their schooling with little or no ability

(Opposite page) A teacher gives individual attention to one of her students. Many illiterate adults are the products of poor or overcrowded educational systems where their problems were not noticed and remedied in time.

One student helps another with her reading. Some students are promoted to the next grade level even though they have not mastered the skills taught at their own grade level.

to read or write. Educators and the public are perplexed by this situation. It is difficult to imagine how any student can graduate from high school unable to read and write. Those who have studied this problem suggest several factors that may help explain how students can complete school without adequate reading and writing skills.

Educational philosophy has played a part in this problem. Until the 1980s teachers frequently promoted students to a higher grade even when the students were not academically ready to move ahead. This technique, called social promotion, was designed to keep students in the same grade as others of their age. The idea behind social promotion was that, as socially promoted students grew older, they would develop the ability to handle their classwork. Meanwhile, they would not have to face the embarrassment of being held back a grade.

Students who totally failed a grade would be made to repeat it. But poor to marginal students who really were not ready for higher-level instruction were moved ahead with their classmates. Some of these students were given special tutoring and eventually were able to build their skills. Many others struggled, receiving the minimum grades needed to pass. These students often fell behind because they had limited reading and writing skills. Thus they had trouble understanding written lessons and completing tests and homework. Those who did not drop out frequently graduated from high school with minimal or no reading or writing abilities. Many illiterate adults today can trace their literacy problems to this method of promotion.

These days students who have trouble in a grade are held back more frequently. However, education experts now are questioning whether this method is better than automatically promoting students based on their age and class attendance. New studies of students who were held back a year or two in school show that they usually do no better than students who could have been held back but were promoted. Indeed, a 1989 article in *NEA Today*, a magazine published by the National Education Association, stated that students who were held back once in their school career dropped out more often than students who were always promoted. Students who were held back twice almost always dropped out of school. This article and others attribute the high number of dropouts to loss of self-esteem in students who are not promoted with their classmates. Staying behind a grade made the students feel that they were stupid and not worthy of higher levels of learning.

Other problems in the classroom

Class size is another obstacle to education. For years teachers and other education experts have known that students in small classes learn better than students in large ones. In smaller classes teachers are able to give students more individual attention. Ideally, no teacher should have more

A teacher tutors two students after school to help them polish their reading skills. Not all students are this fortunate. Many do not receive the help they need and enter the adult world illiterate.

than fifteen students. Unfortunately, this ideal size is impossible to maintain in many school districts. Teachers frequently have to deal with classes of thirty students or more. Some school districts provide assistants to help ease the teacher's burden. In some areas parents may volunteer to help students with lessons, to grade papers, or to do other classroom tasks. But usually the teacher must handle the class alone. As a result, students who have trouble in class may not get as much extra help as they need and thus end up falling behind their classmates.

Teaching methods

Some students also suffer because teachers cannot always tailor their teaching styles to each student's needs. Individuals do not all learn the same way. Education experts have found that there are different ways or styles of learning. Some people learn best by seeing. Some learn by listening. Still others learn by doing. And some learn through a combination of these or other learning styles. Though some schools and some teachers try to accommodate the different learning styles of their students, not all can or do. Many adopt a teaching style that seems to benefit the majority of students. A student who has difficulty learning through that style may fall behind. Teaching expert Marie Carbo has criticized what she says is an "unspoken assumption in our schools: that there is one right way to teach children to read—and that there is something inherently wrong with any student who cannot learn to read by that method."

Education experts such as Carbo have found that using the wrong teaching style for a student almost guarantees that the student will fall behind his or her classmates. Reading programs that "force students to learn [by relying on] their

These students, like students anywhere, do not all learn in the same way. Educators now recognize that a variety of teaching methods helps ensure that most students learn to read.

reading-style weaknesses tend to produce failure, boredom, and loss of self-esteem," Carbo says. Eventually, these students can develop a dislike and fear of reading and learning.

Student learning—and thus literacy—also suffers when schools lack resources and personnel. Schools in poor communities, both urban and rural, struggle more with this problem than in wealthier communities. These schools often have to make do with low budgets, insufficient supplies, low teacher pay, and crowded classrooms. Conditions such as these can dampen enthusiasm and discourage students from completing their education, experts say. Statistics on school dropout rates tend to support this theory. Between October 1990 and October 1991, approximately 400,000 high school students—roughly 3.5 percent of all high school students—dropped out. Sixty percent, or 240,000 of these students, are from the nation's poorest families.

The nation's largest cities provide the most extreme examples of how poor and overburdened schools can discourage young people from learning and, thus, from becoming fully literate. A New York City teenager explained why he dropped out:

I hated school. It was overcrowded. Teachers didn't care. I never knew who my counselor was. After a while, I began spending my time sleeping in class or walking the halls. Finally, I decided to hang out on the streets. That was it. End of school.

For many people literacy begins in the home. Those who are encouraged to read or who grow up in a house filled with books, magazines, and newspapers learn the value and pleasure of reading and writing at an early age. They get a head start on literacy and often read at levels a year or two ahead of their classmates.

Growing up in a family of readers does not guarantee literacy just as growing up with family members who cannot or do not read does not guarantee illiteracy. However, studies suggest that young people whose parents cannot read are at a disadvantage when they begin their own education.

Parents who are illiterate often cannot help their children become literate. Many of these parents feel a sense of pain and helplessness at not being able to participate in this aspect of their children's lives. "I can't read to them," one mother says in *Illiterate America*:

A father reads to his children. Children exposed to books and reading at an early age are often more interested in reading and studying when they begin school.

Of course that's leaving them out of something they should have. . . . The kids belong to a book club. Donny wanted me to read a book to him. . . . I tried it one day, reading from the pictures. Donny looked at me. He said, "Mommy, that's not right." He's only five. He knew I couldn't read.

Feelings of inadequacy or helplessness also keep many illiterate parents from taking an active role in their children's schooling. For these parents school is a reminder of their own failure and they feel powerless to help when they see their children having similar problems. In a 1986 series on illiteracy the *Atlanta Journal* described how parents' illiteracy can affect their children's education:

Illiterate parents often are intimidated by school, so they cannot become activists for their children's education. Many such children live in an environment where reading is not the normal means of getting information. It is something done only in school.

Illiteracy and dyslexia

For millions of Americans illiteracy is a result of neither social nor educational deficiencies. Instead, it is a result of one or more physical conditions that interfere with or wipe out the ability to learn to read and write. Most physical impediments toward becoming literate begin in the brain. The brain is divided into two main sections, one on each side of the skull. In the past century doctors have discovered that each of these sections processes different types of information. In most people the left side of the brain controls language skills, including reading and writing. Specialized groups of brain cells "switch on" when a person reads a book or talks. These cell groups help people attach meaning to the printed or spoken word.

The right half of the brain controls the ability to recognize shapes, maintain sense of direction, and perform other spatial and visual skills. It also lets people understand sights and sounds not related to reading or talking. The right side of the brain allows people to tell the difference between a tall, thin tree and a streetlight, for example. Some people consider the right side to be the more creative side of the brain. Studies have found that great artists and musicians use the right side of their brains more than the left side when working or performing. And art students are encouraged to rely more on the spatially oriented "right brain" than on the more analytical "left brain."

Jumbled letters

In some people, though, both sides of the brain have an equal ability to control the skills of literacy. The two sides of the brain essentially fight each other for control when a person tries to read or write. In the process, the left and right sides of the brain create interfering images of the words a person sees. This interference causes words to appear jumbled. Often, two or more letters in a word will seem to be switched around. *Sit* may appear as *its* or *tis*, for example. Some individual letters may even be reversed, such as the letter S looking like Ƨ.

This interference may also prevent a person from being able to figure out which words or letters are on the page. Sentences might look like clumps of jumbled letters. Some of these letters may seem to change shape on the page as each side of the brain tries to interpret them. Likewise, the reader may see the words and letters perfectly well without being able to tie any meaning to them.

These types of brain-processing problems are grouped together under the term *dyslexia*. Medical researchers and education experts have said that anywhere from 5 to 15 percent of Ameri-

The right half of this young artist's brain governs her ability to recognize images and spatial relationships, and guides her painting. The left half of her brain controls language skills essential for reading and writing.

cans—anywhere from twelve million to thirty-eight million men, women, and children—are dyslexic. Some people with dyslexia never learn the source of their problem and so are forever frustrated by their inability to read. Others, with special training and great personal effort, work around their problems and learn to read. But the problems created by dyslexia never go away. In his book *The Misunderstood Child*, psychiatrist Larry Silver relates how he still has to struggle against his own dyslexia. He described an incident that occurred during a congressional budget hearing. Silver had passed a written note with needed information to someone who was speaking. "When I got my note back, on top it said 'Thanks'—then he proceeded to correct two spelling errors and one [letter] reversal."

Illiteracy is a problem with many causes, some more difficult to understand and solve than others. Indeed, with so many obstacles to the development of literacy, it is easy to understand why there are so many illiterate people.

3

The Costs of Illiteracy

ILLITERACY REACHES DEEP into all aspects of American life. Its effects can be seen in business, in government, and in the home. Illiteracy contributes to workplace and household accidents and influences government policy and spending decisions. But actual costs are difficult to calculate. The American Library Association has estimated that illiteracy costs the nation about $224 billion a year. The Conference Board, a national business organization, has said that American businesses lose roughly $25 billion a year as a result of illiteracy.

Bill Goodling, a U.S. congressman from Pennsylvania, was a member of the House of Representatives' Education and Labor Committee. On this committee he heard firsthand accounts about how illiteracy affected people's lives. Goodling believes that illiteracy is a source of many of America's social ills. "The consequences of illiteracy are devastating for the [illiterate] individuals themselves, for society, and for our economy," he wrote in the Washington, D.C., newspaper *Roll Call*. "Illiteracy has been linked to crime, joblessness, poor school performance, and welfare dependency."

(Opposite page) Two office workers discuss a business document on the job. In today's information-dependent world, the costs of illiteracy become increasingly significant for business, government, and society.

People who cannot read risk injury and even death from misuse of common household chemicals like ammonia. Some manufacturers attach a "Mr. Yuk" sticker to warn those who cannot read about potentially harmful products.

Perhaps the greatest costs are those that cannot be measured in dollars, for illiteracy also exacts a heavy price in human suffering and, at times, in human life.

Illiteracy's costs at home

For a person who cannot read, the home offers many opportunities for disaster. Every day people come into contact with things that seem harmless but could severely injure or kill them. For instance, bleach bottle labels warn that mixing bleach with ammonia or other cleaners will create a poisonous gas. People who cannot read these warnings cannot learn of this danger unless someone else tells them or they hear about it from radio or television. They also cannot understand the instructions and warnings on other household products, medicines, and even some packaged foods.

Researchers and journalists have reported numerous cases of people who have been injured or killed because they could not read warnings like these. The *Atlanta Journal* described one such case, in which a nine-day-old baby died when its mother fed it a bottle of canned formula concentrate. The formula was supposed to be mixed with water before feeding. The label warned that undiluted formula could injure or kill an infant. But the baby's mother could not read this warning or the directions printed on the label. She thus gave her baby a meal that its still-developing body could not handle.

People do not have to be physically hurt to be seriously harmed by their illiteracy, however. In the same article, the *Journal* reported how many illiterate people lost their homes to dishonest business deals. Three hundred homeowners who had fallen behind on their mortgage payments received calls from several real estate companies offering loans that could be used to pay off their mortgages. The homeowners signed what they thought were the papers for these loans but which they later discovered were deeds of sale. They had been tricked into selling their homes to the real estate companies and renting them back from the companies. The loan payments the homeowners thought they were making were actually rent payments.

Although literate people can also fall prey to this type of scheme, an investigation revealed that many of the people in this case were illiterate. They could not read the papers they were told to sign, but they trusted the real estate companies to be honest. An attorney with the Atlanta Legal Aid Society said that this type of swindle is common: "We see dozens of people in here who are victims of their inability to read or write in consumer and real estate transactions."

But people do not need to be swindled to be victimized by their illiteracy. In *Illiterate America* Jonathan Kozol relates the story of a Detroit mother who "brought home a gallon of Crisco for her children's dinner. She thought that she had bought the chicken that was pictured on the label. She had enough Crisco now to last a year—but no more money to go back and buy the food for dinner."

Costs to society

Illiteracy taxes society in less tangible but no less serious ways too. Students who drop out of school before learning to read and write probably never obtain these skills. These young people experience real difficulty making something of their lives. They frequently cannot find work, and if they find work they discover that they qualify only for low-paying jobs. Some give up on finding work altogether; they rely on welfare, food stamps, and other government programs.

Two teenagers work for minimum wage in a fast-food restaurant. Such work is common for students; illiterate adults, however, are often condemned to work in low-paying jobs because their inability to read prevents them from gaining better employment.

Some studies also reveal a link between illiteracy and crime. More than half of this nation's nearly one million prison inmates are semiliterate or functionally illiterate. In California, which has the largest state and federal prison population in the nation, the average prisoner reads at a fifth-grade level or lower. Studies of prisoners under eighteen years old show an even greater rate of illiteracy—eight out of ten are illiterate.

This link between illiteracy and crime leads some experts to conclude that literacy programs might benefit the prison population. Nearly every state has begun testing the literacy skills of its prison inmates. Those who test as illiterate are encouraged—and sometimes ordered by a court—to attend literacy classes. In 1988, for example, the California state legislature passed the Prison Literacy Act. The goal of the act is to give all inmates the opportunity to improve their reading and writing skills. Each state-run prison, under this act, offers adult basic education classes to any prisoner who wishes them.

Anecdotal evidence suggests that literacy programs do benefit prisoners. Literacy workers from Oregon, where 40 percent of prisoners read

An ex-convict studies to improve his literacy skills. Having better reading and writing ability improves his chances of staying out of prison.

below the eighth-grade level, to Texas, where roughly three out of every four prisoners are illiterate, say their programs work. "They come in not wanting to be here because they are court-ordered. But then you see the change. After they start learning and see that they can achieve, their self-esteem rises and they blossom," said Danna Huddleston, a literacy instructor for a Travis County, Texas, program.

Youthful inmates in a New York house of detention spend time in the library improving their literacy skills. Achieving literacy raises self-esteem and motivates people to learn.

Prisons of the mind

Some prison reformers and education experts also hope that literacy programs will help reduce crime. By giving inmates the basic skills needed to survive outside prison, they suggest that the inmates will have a greater chance of finding work and staying out of jail when they are released. However, some prison officials have said that increasing an inmate's literacy skills does not guarantee that the person will turn away from crime.

A woman fills out a ballot at a voting booth. Voting is a right enjoyed by American citizens. Many illiterate people shy away from exercising this right.

The California Department of Corrections, in a 1988 report to the state legislature, said that there is "only a slight correlation between higher reading levels" and former prisoners staying out of jail.

While many people who commit crimes have limited literacy skills, many more people with this problem never turn to crime. In another sense, though, these people are imprisoned by their inability to read and write. Generally, people who cannot read do not take an active part in society. Their illiteracy drains them of personal and political power. They cannot learn for themselves about the history and politics of their city, state, or nation. Even voting, with its printed ballots and multiple choices, becomes a major challenge. "I tried to vote once, and it was disastrous," said one Oregon man, a participant in the state's literacy program. "I've never tried again."

In *Illiteracy: An American Dilemma* David Harman spelled out some of the values that literacy offers beyond its functional applications. The most important of these values, he said, is the intellectual freedom that literacy provides. Being able to read allows people the freedom to decide what they want or need to learn. If they can read, they can seek this knowledge for themselves. Literacy, Harman said, allows people "to determine for themselves what they wish to know, and in what depth. . . . It enables people to transcend the boundaries set by others."

Kings and dictators have always feared the power of knowledge. For this reason European monarchs and clergy in the Middle Ages controlled the printed word. As a result, information about the world was restricted to the ruling classes. In this way they hoped to keep the common people from questioning the established order. The idea of keeping people ignorant by keeping them illiterate was alive in seventeenth-century America, too. Sir William Berkeley, the British governor of colonial Virginia, was said to have opposed teaching the entire population to read. Doing so, he said, might expose the colonists to ideas of self-government and lead them to rebel against England. Dictators in more recent times have also tried to restrict the literacy of their citizens. Like authoritarian rulers before them, they know and fear the power that knowledge brings.

An engineer reads plans for a new project. Workers who cannot read, write, and count beyond grade-school levels will hurt America's future.

The workplace

One of the more pressing problems facing the United States is a gradual decrease in the number of literate workers. Nearly two million students leave school each year—either by graduating or by dropping out—without being able to read or write above an eight-grade level. Employers in all fields, from fast-food restaurants to textile plants, have seen thousands of job applicants who are not qualified for entry-level work because they cannot read or write as well as a high school freshman.

In 1987 the chairman of Xerox Corporation, David Kearns, said that businesses will be forced to hire workers with poor literacy skills to replace employees or to expand company operations:

> American businesses will have to hire more than a million new service and production workers a year who can't read, write or count. Teaching them how and absorbing the lost productivity while they are learning will cost industry $25 billion a year for as long as it takes.

In addition to training new employees, businesses will have to retrain longtime employees who have managed to get by with low levels of literacy. These older employees, hired at a time when literacy was not a major concern, are a small but significant part of the nation's work force. There is no exact count of how many people fall into this group. But as in the rest of society, workers who are totally illiterate are a small part of the problem. A 1990 study for the Conference Board found that a majority of workers with low levels of literacy can read and write simple sentences, but not much more.

Poor skills

The report also said that some companies already are seeing an increase in the number of illiterate people coming into the work force. Major manufacturing and service firms have to interview hundreds, occasionally thousands, of applicants to find qualified workers. For example, Southwestern Bell, a regional telephone company, needed to hire new workers in the late 1980s. More than fifteen thousand people applied for the positions offered, which required a range of skills. But an initial screening showed that only thirty-seven hundred of these applicants could read and write well enough to be considered for the available jobs. And of these thirty-seven hundred, only eight hundred passed a basic skills test. In other words, only five people out of

every hundred who originally applied for work could read and write well enough to be considered for a job.

Training these new workers and longtime employees to read has become crucial. Businesses around the country have switched to more advanced methods of operation that require more on-the-job reading than in the past. "For instance," a literacy program director says in an *Arkansas Democrat* newspaper article, "you've got computer printouts in manufacturing and distribution plants . . . [where before] it was just a foreman telling you where to move that stack of pallets."

When companies have workers who read and write poorly, they lose money. Illiterate workers tend to learn tasks slowly, since they cannot read instruction manuals. They do not know their jobs as well as they would if they could read, and they tend to make more on-the-job mistakes. Some-

Business employees today must be able to read computer printouts, flowcharts, and other written data. Poor readers learn their jobs more slowly, have more on-the-job accidents, and make more mistakes than colleagues who read well.

Auto mechanics and others who work mostly with their hands read computer printouts and sophisticated repair and instruction manuals as part of their jobs.

times these mistakes cost thousands of dollars. In one case a night janitor ruined a floor he was supposed to polish when he used the wrong bottle of chemicals. Until then he had held on to his job by getting a friend to read labels and instructions to him. On that night, though, his friend was off work, and he was forced to guess which bottle contained the polish. Ranch hands and feedlot workers have killed whole herds of cattle accidentally by feeding them poison instead of cattle food. After one such accident, a ranch hand admitted "I wasn't real sure what the package said."

Sometimes the results of a worker's mistakes are even more tragic. A Pennsylvania business journal told how illiteracy killed a factory worker. According to a literacy expert from Pennsylvania State University, the worker had gone into an unoccupied room for a cigarette. He did not know that the room contained explosive chemicals and fumes, because he could not read warning signs that said "DANGER: NO SMOKING." When he lit his cigarette, the explosion that resulted killed him instantly.

Shared responsibility

Accidents like these are why illiteracy in the workplace is so costly. While the cost in human lives can never be made up, the cost in lost production time and damaged machinery is passed on to consumers. However, some economists and business experts are beginning to say that the issue of illiteracy is being used to mask poor business practices. Recent reports on worker productivity suggest that illiteracy is not a threat to American industry. Despite claims made in the 1970s and 1980s about the supposed inefficiency of the American work force, American workers actually outperform workers in other nations. This result prompted Jonathan Weisman, a reporter for the *San Jose Business Journal*, to suggest that business executives have been using the issue of illiteracy as a way to draw attention away from bad business practices. Weisman presented a similar conclusion from economists from around the nation, such as Stanford University economics professor Henry Levin, who said:

> The easiest way [for executives] to take pressure off of themselves for producing a lousy product . . . is to say "How can we [improve] it? We have a lousy work force!". . . This is basically a (rotten) excuse for a lousy management process.

4

Literacy Programs in Other Nations

ILLITERACY IS NOT just an American problem. Nor is it a problem only of the 1990s. Illiteracy has challenged the leadership of many nations for many decades, though it has challenged some more than others.

Nations that have tried to eliminate illiteracy have met with varying degrees of success. Some of them have managed to virtually eliminate illiteracy after decades of work. Others have reached many fewer people and made much less of a difference. The most successful literacy efforts have featured extensive government involvement and clearly defined goals.

Though these literacy drives usually started as ten-year programs, most had to be extended before they showed any real progress. Some nations were faced with huge numbers of people who could neither read nor write. Other nations were so poor and had such rudimentary education systems that even small successes could be considered victories. But those nations that have persisted with their literacy efforts have been able to teach a majority of their citizens to read and write.

(Opposite page) A group of women from a Nigerian village attend a literacy class. People in nations around the world recognize the greater opportunities available to those who can read and write.

Establishing successful literacy programs in poor nations is a big challenge. Limited resources require these Pakistani schoolgirls to share books and a single wooden bench.

One of the most ambitious national literacy drives took place in the Soviet Union more than sixty years ago. From 1917 to 1921 a communist revolution and civil war overthrew the government of the Russian Empire, bringing a patchwork of republics under the banner of the Soviet Union. The leader of this revolution, Vladimir Lenin, vowed to create a government in which all citizens shared equally in both the labor and fruits of the system. This had not been the case under the czars, or emperors, who had ruled the Russian Empire for so many years.

The 100 million people who were united as one nation after the revolution were mostly poor, uneducated peasants. They spoke as many as 122 different languages. Few, however, knew how to read or write in any language, either in their native tongue or in Russian, which had become the common language. More than 70 million people, or 70 percent of the population, were completely illiterate. For the Soviet Union to grow technologically and culturally in the twentieth century, Lenin and others believed, citizens needed to possess basic reading and writing skills. They also hoped to hasten the acceptance of the new communist political and social system, as well as the melding of the various nationalities and linguistic groups, through a literacy program.

The Soviet literacy drive

To meet these goals Lenin ordered a massive educational program to begin on December 26, 1919. The program's goal was to wipe out illiteracy by 1927, the tenth anniversary of the revolution that overthrew the government and put the Communist Party in power. Lenin intended for every Soviet citizen to be able to read and write at least at a fourth- or fifth-grade level. In his declaration creating this literacy drive, Lenin said:

> All the population of the Republic between the ages of eight and fifty who are unable to read and write must learn to do so in their own language or in Russian, as they wish. This instruction will be given in state schools, both those already existing and those being set up for the illiterate population under the plans of the People's Commissariat [Department] for Education.

Lenin's plan called for literate citizens of the new Soviet Union to volunteer as reading and writing tutors and thus share the burden with the nation's teachers. The plan also gave local literacy commissions, called People's Commissariats of Enlightenment, the power to draft literate citizens as tutors. All the work done by these volunteers and professionals was controlled by the central government through its education department.

The Soviet literacy drive was one of the largest national social programs ever attempted. H. S. Bhola, who wrote about various literacy campaigns in his book *Campaigning for Literacy*, explained the huge scale of the task Lenin had taken on:

A 1920 Soviet poster encourages literacy. It proclaims, "An illiterate is the same as a blind man—failure and unhappiness await him everywhere."

It was . . . the first attempt by a state to make all its people literate—men and women, rural and urban, workers and peasants, speaking more than a hundred tongues, spread over half a continent constituting the largest country in the world.

The literacy program included a mass publicity campaign to convince the public to take part. Newly literate workers spoke at factory meetings about the ways their lives had improved. Signs and banners encouraging literacy were posted in the cities. The government even produced a play called "How Ugly to Be Illiterate" and showed it in the larger cities.

The officials in charge of the program, including Lenin, said that the population needed to read and write to keep the Soviet Union technologically and culturally active in the twentieth century. But the campaign had an ulterior motive—to expose the population to the communist ideology of the nation's new government. By melding the various nationalities and linguistic groups into one culture, Lenin hoped, the process of political education would be made easier.

Lenin was determined to see the literacy drive succeed and was not willing to leave its success to chance. In an effort to ensure its success, Lenin made it illegal for any person who was illiterate

A student in a Russian school recites a lesson. Education, and especially literacy, were high priorities in the Soviet Union.

to refuse to learn to read and write. It also was against the law for any literate person to refuse to teach these skills. Despite Lenin's efforts, many people did resist the government's insistence that they learn to read and write. Some people simply felt that if their parents and grandparents could live without learning to read, they could too.

Nor did the program go as smoothly or as quickly as Lenin had hoped. There were delays and other problems in setting up the nationwide system of literacy instructors and providing books and other materials. The program had to be extended for another ten years when the deadline Lenin had imposed for achieving literacy slipped by without the Soviet Union's reaching the goal.

Nevertheless, in 1939 the government announced that more than 87 percent of the population had acquired basic literacy skills. Greater levels of literacy were encouraged and, eventually, literacy levels rose even higher. Today, in what are now the republics of the former Soviet Union, almost all 290 million people can read at the high school level or higher.

Passers-by stop outside the offices of the Moscow News *to read the latest headlines. Decades of compulsory literacy programs gave the Soviet Union one of the highest literacy rates in the world.*

China

The People's Republic of China followed the Soviet Union's lead in literacy drives soon after the Chinese communist revolution of 1949. China had even fewer literate people than did the Soviet Union. Out of a population of 550 million, only 83 million, or 15 percent, could read or write. Most of these literate Chinese lived in major cities. People living in the rural areas had few, if any, nearby schools. In any case, these farmers, fishermen, and other laborers were usually too poor to pay for educating their children.

With nearly 470 million people unable to read or write, a single, centrally run program was not possible. Instead, each community formed its own literacy organization and set up its own methods of education. The government provided guidelines and materials to aid their efforts. Local literacy committees also were responsible for bringing people into the program.

Like the Soviet Union, China was a land of many languages. In 1949 eight or nine separate languages were spoken throughout the nation. However, only one system of writing was used for all these languages. Instead of an alphabet with a set number of letters, Chinese writing uses thousands of different characters that represent whole ideas, such as "house," "wind," or "woman." To be literate, a person needed to know around fifteen hundred of these characters.

The Chinese government took three steps to make learning these characters easier and, at the same time, to give the country a single language. It declared that one dialect, Mandarin, was the official language of China and eliminated words that were not in widespread use. It simplified the design of a number of the written characters. And it invented a Western-style alphabet—one that expresses sounds rather than ideas—to help people remember the characters and their pronunciation.

Difficult circumstances

In the years since the program began, China has gone through a slow but dramatic turnaround in its literacy rate. In the first ten years, sixty-eight million people graduated from literacy classes. By the mid-1980s the literacy rate had risen to 70 percent. China's population now numbers more than one billion people. Roughly 345 million of this population cannot read. About 91 percent, or 313 million, of the illiterate Chinese live in rural regions. In 1990 the government began a new program to expand literacy classes in these regions. The government hopes to eventually bring the literacy rate up to 90 percent.

Not every country that attempts to raise its level of literacy succeeds this well, however. Circumstances—economic, political, even cultural—can hamper drives for literacy. For example, until the late 1970s Ethiopia had an illiteracy rate of 93 percent. Only 2.25 million people out of Ethiopia's population of 32 million could read and write even simple sentences. While illiteracy was a major problem for Ethiopia, it was just one of many serious problems troubling this impoverished nation. Lack of water and extreme food shortages caused by drought killed hundreds of thousands of people. And violent uprisings against the nation's military government repeatedly shook the nation.

Even so, in 1979 the government set up more than thirty-four thousand literacy learning centers in towns and villages throughout the country. Roughly 250,000 tutors were hired to work in these centers. By 1985 the number of literate Ethiopians had increased to more than 7.5 million, nearly 18 percent of a population of 42,250,000. These advances came to a halt in the early 1980s. A series of severe droughts, followed by the overthrow of the government in 1991, has devastated Ethiopia and effectively ended the country's drive for literacy.

Nicaragua

Sometimes a largely successful campaign against illiteracy also can be used as a tool for greater social understanding. In 1979 a revolutionary group called the Sandinista National Liberation Front overthrew the government of Nicaragua, a nation in Central America. Once in power, the Sandinistas began a literacy program designed to teach people about the new political order while they were learning to read and write.

Nicaraguan students show interest in the subject they are reading about. The Sandinista government set up literacy programs as a means to help the people learn about the new social and political order in their country.

As part of a literacy campaign, a high school student from Managua, Nicaragua's capital city, teaches a girl living in a rural area how to read and write.

Of the roughly two million citizens of Nicaragua, half were considered functionally illiterate. Most of these people lived in rural areas of the nation, where there were few schools.

The Nicaraguan literacy campaign, which began in 1980, provided ninety thousand literacy tutors to teach in the country and in city neighborhoods with large populations of illiterate adults. The methods the program used were hailed by literacy experts around the world. Rural tutors, mostly young adults in their teens and twenties, lived with farming families, working in the fields in the day and teaching at night. Not only did the farmers benefit from their literacy instruction, but the mostly city-raised young tutors learned what life was like for the majority of Nicaragua's working poor.

The campaign took another tack to bring literacy to illiterate city dwellers. City literacy classes took place in settings that their students were familiar with—such as churches, office buildings, even marketplaces and a brewery—rather than in formal school buildings. The teachers for these classes were mostly factory workers, housewives, and other literate adult Nicaraguans, who could relate easily to their older urban students.

For a small country like Nicaragua the program was a big success. By the end of the first year of the program, Nicaraguan officials estimated, more than 400,000 people had learned basic literacy skills. And by 1985 nearly 2 million out of a population of 2.25 million people could read and write. The scope and the methods used in the campaign earned Nicaragua the UNESCO (United Nations Educational, Scientific, and Cultural Organization) Literacy Award in the early 1980s.

An international boost

Despite successes in improving literacy, as in the Soviet Union and Nicaragua, the overall world illiteracy rate has risen steadily for most of the century. In 1970 the United Nations estimated that there were 890 million illiterate, or at best semiliterate, adults over fifteen years old. In 1990 the United Nations found that the number of illiterate adults had increased to 948 million. In other words, of all the adults in the world, more than one out of four cannot read or write.

There has been some good news, however. UNESCO estimates that the number of adult illiterates in the world will drop to 942 million by the year 2,000. There are signs that this decrease is already under way. The 926 million illiterate adults in 1990 actually represent a drop of 2 million from the illiterate population in 1987, one of the first decreases in the illiterate population on

A woman from the Middle Eastern nation of Yemen participates in a United Nations-sponsored world literacy program. Such worldwide efforts are steadily reducing the world illiteracy rate.

record. While these facts are encouraging, UNESCO says they are proof that the battle against illiteracy is going "painfully slow."

A year for literacy

In an attempt to speed up the fight, the United Nations decided to support a worldwide literacy campaign throughout the 1990s. The United Nations, working mainly through UNESCO, has provided literacy training, helped build or repair school buildings, and given money and awards to literacy programs around the world. In its latest effort the United Nations began helping countries plan, promote, and in some cases pay for, new or improved literacy programs. Most of this work is focused on developing nations in Africa, Central and South America, the Caribbean, and parts of Southeast Asia. The United Nations also has extended its own literacy work through its food, health, labor, and other allied organizations. For example, the World Health Organization is pro-

Adult Illiterates (Age 15 and Over) and Illiteracy Rates

	Adult Illiterates (in millions)			Illiteracy Rates (%)			Decrease 1985-2000
	1985	1990	2000	1985	1990	2000	% Points
World Total	965.1	962.6	942.0	29.9	26.9	22.0	-7.9
Developing Countries	908.1	920.6	918.5	39.4	35.1	28.1	-11.3
Developed Countries	57.0	42.0	23.5	6.2	4.4	2.3	-3.9

Source: UNESCO

A literacy class in the north African nation of Tunisia teaches these women to write in both Arabic and English. The class is part of a United Nations educational effort begun in 1990.

viding reading instruction as part of its efforts to teach people about health and hygiene.

The United Nations and many individual countries—China, for example—kicked off this new wave of literacy programs in 1990. They announced their new proliteracy strategies in a year-long series of conferences and media events called the International Literacy Year. The International Literacy Year was also designed to encourage nations with large illiteracy rates to improve efforts to educate their people. An immediate improvement in the number of adults who become literate is unlikely, as it takes years for large-scale change in a population to occur. But the organizers of the literacy year were looking toward the long-term effect of their efforts. They hoped that, by providing this boost to international literacy, they could reduce the number of illiterate adults at the beginning of the next century.

5

Achieving Literacy in the United States

AMERICA SEEMS TO be in a far better position to educate its illiterate population than are other nations. The United States economy is relatively strong, and the country has an essentially stable political and social system. It even has a larger base of literate citizens than do many other countries. Yet the nation has been unable to reduce the number of illiterate people, despite decades of government-sponsored and private programs.

Perhaps the biggest obstacle to a successful American literacy movement is the on-and-off interest the public takes in the problem. Illiteracy rises to the center of public attention only to fade and then rise again. Thomas G. Sticht, the president of a sociological research firm, spoke to Congress during a series of hearings on illiteracy in 1985. "Illiteracy is a recurringly discovered problem," he said, "usually pushed into national prominence by war, cultural upheaval and economic crisis." Each of these events provides a stage upon which America's social ills can be highlighted. During social conflicts more atten-

(Opposite page) A volunteer tutors a young man in basic reading and writing skills. Literacy program volunteers are an important part of the fight against illiteracy in America.

tion is paid to the people who are at the bottom of society and who suffer most from these up-heavals. Because most illiterate adults are in this group, their plight is more widely publicized than at times of relative ease.

Each time the public rediscovers illiteracy, Sticht said, people feel compelled to stamp it out as if it was a fire in a wheat field. They pressure the government to set short-term goals for defeating illiteracy. The new programs created to satisfy these demands often try to teach every illiterate adult to read and write in no more than a decade. Then, when the public sees that illiteracy cannot be solved that easily, it loses interest until the next time it hears of the "illiteracy crisis." In general, the history of twentieth-century literacy work mirrors the start-and-stop interest the American public has shown in the problem.

"Say, Buddy, you got any idea where the Illiterate Club is?"

The American public first became aware of widespread adult illiteracy after World War I. The United States Army had tested the reading and writing skills of recruits. The results of these tests surprised many policy makers and the public. The army found that most recruits could not read at fourth-grade level. Politicians and others urged improved public education to raise literacy levels. Most people, though, were more concerned with putting the war behind them. Europe's industrial decline following the war helped create a booming economy in the United States, and the public's interest in prosperity outweighed its interest in illiteracy.

New awareness

In the thirty years that followed the booming 1920s, a few literacy programs were created around the nation. Many of these programs were local responses to the Great Depression of the 1930s, a means of helping unemployed illiterate adults improve their chances of finding work. Illiteracy received little public attention, though, until the 1960s. During this decade social concerns about racial injustice, poverty, and educational equality became a major focus of public attention. Civil rights and social change gained status as national priorities. For the first time much of the general public realized how many people had been left behind in America's rapid rise as a modern, progressive, industrialized society.

This new awareness prompted the federal government and many state legislatures to create programs to eliminate social inequality in its many forms. These programs were designed to fulfill the idea of America as being, in the words of President Lyndon Johnson, a "Great Society." One of the first of these programs was established under the Economic Opportunity Act of 1964. As part of a general welfare package, this law gave money to a nationwide system of community-based literacy classes. Many of these classes were set up in high schools, community centers, or community colleges and were run like regular school classes. The government hoped these classes would help illiterate adults improve their lives.

Another law attempted to give children of low-income families a better chance to become literate. Part of the Elementary and Secondary Education Act of 1965 gave schools money to improve the quality of education available to low-income children. Education experts saw that illiteracy was both a cause and a result of poverty. They believed that improved levels of education and literacy would help children break free of the poverty-illiteracy cycle.

Right to Read

The drive for national literacy did benefit from these laws and from other similar acts that were passed afterward. Some illiterate adults did learn to read and write, and some children were able to gain a better education. But none of these programs came even close to meeting the goal of eradicating illiteracy in America. All the money the government gave to fight adult illiteracy added up to one dollar for every person who needed the help these programs provided. Supplemental contributions from state and local government added only two or three dollars per person. With so little money available, government literacy programs were unable to help more than a couple of million people each year—at most, 4 percent of the nation's illiterate and semiliterate adult population.

One of the government-sponsored literacy programs of this period was called Right to Read. Started in 1971, Right to Read took its name from

A literacy volunteer uses newspaper employment ads to teach reading and to help her student look for a job.

a speech made by James Allen, the commissioner of education in the late 1960s. Allen declared that every American had the right to read no matter what his or her family background. He said that America should work to wipe out illiteracy by 1980. In hopes of reaching that goal, the federal government spent up to five million dollars a year on a nationwide network of reading academies. A majority of this money was spent on community-based reading programs that were not concerned with meeting some theoretical statewide or national literacy standard. Instead, they focused on practical applications of literacy, teaching only the skills their students needed in everyday life.

Right to Read did help illiterate and semiliterate people gain and improve reading and writing skills. It did not achieve its goal of total literacy by the end of the decade, however. Eight years into its ten-year mission, the director of Right to Read, Gilbert Schiffman, called the program a failure. Some observers said the program had received too little money to achieve its ambitious goals. Others said the program's goals were unrealistic from the start.

Students in an adult education class work on their writing skills. In 1992, the federal government gave nearly two billion dollars to vocational and adult education programs, including literacy training.

Much of the problem with government programs like Right to Read is that the people who put them together need to convince the government to pay for them. And to get the money, they have to convince the government that these programs can meet their goals of full national literacy. But the goals these programs try to meet turn out to be unreachable. "Such goals are rhetoric," said researchers Carman St. John Hunter and David Harman, "designed to secure legislation and funding from a Congress that knows little about its educationally and economically marginal constituents."

The members of Congress find themselves in a bind over illiteracy. They do not want to seem insensitive to the problems that illiterate people face. But they also do not want to be seen wasting money on programs that have no hope of fulfilling their promise. A single, decades-long literacy effort costing billions of dollars is sure to be unpopular. As a result, Congress has approved compromise plans that show concern about the problem yet do not pay enough or do enough to solve it.

A fresh attempt at national literacy

The need for some national effort to reduce illiteracy has kept the federal government involved in a number of areas. As in the past, some of its efforts involve handing out money to literacy programs around the nation. Some of this money goes to state education departments, which pass it on to local education programs, sometimes with additional money from state taxes. The federal government also runs its own vocational and adult education programs, which themselves feature literacy training. During the 1980s money for vocational and adult education amounted to roughly $1 billion a year. Government funding in this area rose to about $1.9 billion in 1992.

Literacy programs do not get all of this money, however. At most, federal and state literacy grants amount to $450 for each literacy student. Most literacy programs require much more. For example, a mid-1980s study by Harvard University found that Massachusetts literacy centers spent as much as $2,500 for each student they enrolled. This money paid for literacy tutors and teaching materials, as well as for electricity, furniture, and other operating costs. To make up the difference, these centers often spent a great deal of time raising money from private foundations.

Although most discussions about illiteracy get down to money—how much is available and how it should be spent—other issues enter the debate. One such issue is what to do about the fragmented nature of literacy programs. Most programs have a common goal—that is, improving literacy. But these programs often operate in isolation from each other. Lack of a coordinated approach, or at least a means of sharing information and resources, leads to overlap in some areas and holes in others.

In an effort to correct this situation and strengthen literacy efforts across the nation, Congress passed the National Literacy Act, which President George Bush signed into law in 1991. The National Literacy Act called for the creation of a National Institute for Literacy. As planned, this institute would act as a clearinghouse through which literacy program administrators and workers around the nation could communicate. It would serve as the headquarters for federal literacy programs, including literacy grants. It would also support a number of regional resource centers that would provide even more rapid communication and support for programs in their areas.

In addition, the National Literacy Act called for increased spending on literacy programs. The act set aside $1.1 billion to be spent from 1992 to 1995. The act also contains plans for helping small businesses set up their own literacy programs, distributing free books to children from low-income families, and supporting library-based literacy classes.

Libraries and literacy instruction

Government literacy programs are not the only methods American society has used to fight illiteracy. Perhaps this country's oldest advocates of nationwide literacy are its libraries. From 1820 to 1920 America was the destination of thousands of European immigrants. Many of these people were literate in their native languages but few spoke or read much, if any, English.

Libraries, especially those in cities with large immigrant populations like New York, Boston, and Chicago, took up the challenge of making these new American citizens literate in English. They offered classes aimed at helping immigrants improve their English. They expanded their collection of foreign-language books, both to encourage immigrants to use the library and to attract them to the English classes. Some libraries even hired English-speaking immigrants as assistants, to make sure their potential students knew about the services the libraries offered. Soon libraries became centers of learning second only to the public schools.

For a while after 1920 some libraries continued to offer classes for adults who needed to learn how to read and write. But these classes did not last when the Great Depression hit in the 1930s.

President George Bush and Barbara Bush (center) pose with honorees recognized for their efforts in improving literacy in the United States. In 1991, Bush signed the National Literacy Act, which called for the establishment of a National Literacy Institute.

A library worker electronically checks out a book for a patron. Public libraries have traditionally been at the forefront of efforts to raise literacy levels in the United States.

Libraries in general did not take an active role in literacy training again until the 1960s and 1970s. As part of the Great Society government programs initiated during that period, the American Library Association began teaching librarians how to set up and run literacy programs. Libraries in large cities developed their own classes, helping people who could read a little improve their skills as well as teaching those with no literacy skills how to read and write. By the early 1980s one out of every two public libraries offered some sort of literacy program.

Library literacy programs are not really much different from other literacy programs. They usually consist of specially trained tutors teaching one student at a time. Hattie McGowan, a North

Carolina volunteer library literacy tutor, describes how the process worked with one fifty-year-old student:

> The first few lessons were spent getting acquainted and gaining his confidence. Some nonreaders are embarrassed at first, and it is so important to convey your sincere feelings that you are here by choice to help them. Once a modicum of rapport is established, it becomes easier and the student relaxes. . . . It was touching to see his excitement build up when he would learn a few new words; he couldn't believe it was happening to him.

Many library literacy programs receive federal and often state support as part of the government's library services programs. In 1992 the U.S. Department of Education distributed more than $105 million to support library services, including literacy classes.

Private volunteer programs

A great number of nonlibrary volunteer programs and literacy organizations also have been working to decrease the national illiteracy rate.

A volunteer tutor from Literacy Volunteers of America, a private national literacy association founded in 1962, works with his pupil. The tutor teaches reading skills with the help of a newspaper.

Some of these groups are small and are run by charitable groups or local governments. Others are part of private or church-based literacy associations that maintain their own programs around the nation. All together, these programs teach reading, writing, and other skills to roughly 300,000 students each year.

The two oldest and most prominent of the national associations are Laubach Literacy Action and Literacy Volunteers of America (commonly known as LVA). Laubach Literacy Action is a branch of a larger organization, Laubach Literacy International, that has been in existence since 1955. Literacy Volunteers of America was founded in 1962. Both groups operate networks of literacy tutors throughout America. Most of these tutors are volunteers who are trained by the parent organizations. They teach their students, using materials and methods from the parent organizations. Combined, these groups supervise more than 375,000 students and tutors each year.

Even the White House has become involved in illiteracy in recent years. During her early years as First Lady, Barbara Bush lent her name to an organization that supports literacy efforts aimed

A volunteer tutor from Laubach Literacy Action, a privately funded, national network of tutors, helps a student with his lessons. Private literacy associations offer much-needed services to those who wish to improve their reading skills.

at teaching entire families to read. The Barbara Bush Foundation for Family Literacy gives grants to state and county governments, volunteer literacy projects, and medical centers that provide family literacy programs. In 1992 the foundation awarded $500,000 to thirteen organizations, with individual awards ranging from $14,000 to $50,000

First Lady Barbara Bush poses with three youngsters at a 1989 White House luncheon during which she launched the Barbara Bush Foundation for Family Literacy. The foundation provides grants to literacy programs around the country.

Private business and industry programs

In recent years national and local literacy organizations have been joined by business and media groups that support literacy projects. A good deal of this support has come from newspapers, magazine and book publishers, book sellers, and broadcasting companies. Part of their involvement is philanthropic, coming from a desire to help people in need. But they also share a strong business reason for their involvement. Declining literacy in the work force and among consumers threatens their livelihoods.

There are a number of ways these industries have contributed their time and money. Harold McGraw Jr., a former chairman of the McGraw-Hill publishing house, founded a business literacy group using $1 million of his own money in 1983. This group, the Business Council for Effective Literacy, started its work by giving a public-service advertising group, the Ad Council, $400,000 to develop a national literacy awareness campaign. It helped support the American Library Association's Coalition for Literacy, a program started in the early 1980s to develop library-based literacy programs. It also encourages or lobbies federal and state legislatures to pass literacy and school reform legislation.

There are other ways in which businesses have contributed to literacy efforts. B. Dalton Booksellers, a national bookstore chain, runs the National Literacy Initiative, a program that donates money to community literacy projects. And Capital Cities Broadcasting, the owners of the ABC television network, has sponsored proliteracy and proeducation television ads since 1986 through its group Project Learning U.S., or PLUS.

Extra help for workers

Other businesses are slowly beginning to fight illiteracy in the nation's work force. Some companies are offering literacy programs in the workplace. Workers can attend classes in meeting rooms or employee lounges, usually before or after work. These in-house programs also help employees develop problem-solving and communication skills. Other companies send employees to community literacy or adult education programs for help in improving their reading and writing skills.

But in-house literacy programs are not found in many companies. A 1990 report on work-force illiteracy by the Conference Board, said that only 10 percent of this nation's companies provide worker literacy programs. The companies that offer such programs are usually ones with thousands of workers, such as automobile makers, insurance companies, and electronics companies.

Some of these programs are designed to raise the level of education in general among their employees. For example, at Hershey Foods, the Pennsylvania food company, workers who did not graduate from high school take classes that prepare them to take the state's graduate equivalency exam. Since 1984 the company has provided tutors in math and science, as well as reading and writing. Students who cannot read above a fifth-grade level are sent to a county industrial literacy group, which provides professional tutors.

The classes these companies provide usually are for newly hired workers with borderline read-

Capital Cities Broadcasting helps to promote literacy and education through its group Project Learning U.S., or PLUS.

ing and writing skills. Some companies and industry groups, however, are developing literacy-improvement projects for longtime employees. These classes will be designed to help workers improve their positions in a company or change jobs if it becomes necessary.

But how well does it work?

Literacy programs of all types have helped many people learn to read and write over the years. Despite the millions of dollars spent on governmental, privately run, and company-based literacy programs in America, no one knows exactly how many people manage to become literate each year. Although many people complete their literacy classes, many others drop out before learning to read and write. Illiterate adults sometimes have difficulty balancing jobs, family, *and* literacy classes. Others find out that learning to read and write takes months, even years, of practice, and simply lose interest.

For those who do become literate, there usually is no means of finding out if their new knowledge actually helps them improve their lives. There is virtually no follow-up or tracking of former students to see which methods work and which do not. Instead of focusing on how well people do after they go through a literacy program, literacy programs are more concerned about the number of people who have yet to join. "Today," Forrest P. Chisman said in *Leadership for Literacy*, "literacy service in America is almost entirely input-driven." Budgets are made based on "the number of learners to be served, the number of hours of service, the cost of materials," and other expenses related to maintaining the program itself. The actual results of the program wind up being pushed out of the spotlight.

Literacy experts are pointing out the need for some sort of accountability in the nation's literacy programs, given the millions of dollars spent on them each year. Speaking about company-based literacy programs in an interview with the *Los Angeles Times*, Chisman said "We need to know whether we are succeeding or failing. I am astounded how some of these companies put out substantial amounts of money and do not know if they are getting their money's worth."

6

Literacy Beyond Reading and Writing

FOR MOST OF the twentieth century, discussions of literacy have focused on skills with words. Occasionally, literacy experts have expanded their views to include basic math skills, such as those needed to balance a checkbook or to plan a monthly budget. Many literacy programs do, in fact, include some mathematics lessons as part of their goal of teaching people how to function fully in society. In general, though, to be literate means having skills in reading and writing and using these skills in everyday life.

But in the past five or ten years, some educators and researchers have suggested a need to change this common definition. The complexities of modern life, they say, require a broader view of literacy, one that goes beyond just being able to read a job ad or take a driver's license test. Individuals have to have a store of basic information—about history, geography, politics, and so on—in order to fully understand the events that surround and shape their lives. They need this shared body of knowledge so they can communi-

(Opposite page) Achieving a high level of literacy entails more than mastering basic reading and writing skills. These skills are only the first steps on a lifelong journey of learning.

cate easily with each other. At the same time, in order to comprehend rapid scientific and technological developments, people have to be familiar with numbers and mathematical relationships.

The need for this new view of literacy, experts say, can be seen in the results of a number of studies of American students' academic performance. In one study during the mid-1980s, the National Science Foundation and the U.S. Department of Education compared math ability in American thirteen-year-olds with that of students in Canada, England, Ireland, South Korea, and Spain. Students from the United States scored last among the six countries. Other studies have shown a similar lack of knowledge in American students about geography, history, English, and other subjects.

One of the most surprising examples of this lack of knowledge came in a study by E.D. Hirsch, an English professor at the University of Virginia. Hirsch asked a group of Richmond, Virginia, community college students to read a passage about the American Civil War. The passage discussed the surrender of the Confederate commanding general, Robert E. Lee, to the Union general, Ulysses S. Grant, at the end of the war. The study revealed that, despite the importance of the Civil War—and the fact that Richmond had been the capital city of the Confederacy—none of the college students knew who Grant or Lee was.

Cultural literacy

Hirsch is one of the educators who have been calling for an expanded view of literacy as part of a general reform of the nation's education system. In his 1987 book, *Cultural Literacy: What Every American Needs to Know*, Hirsch suggested that American schools need to teach a common curriculum that gives each student a lifelong familiarity with art, science, literature, politics, history—in short, with the basic facts of America's cultural heritage.

Hirsch suggested the term *cultural literacy* to describe the basic knowledge that all individuals should have. He described cultural literacy as "the network of information that all competent readers possess." For instance, a person reading a newspaper about a congressional investigation into bank fraud should already know that Congress is the branch of government that makes and passes laws and that banks and other institutions are regulated by the government.

Earlier in this century, Hirsch said, most students who graduated from high school not only had been taught these basic facts, but also how they relate to each other. But in the past twenty to

Hands-on experience in the biology laboratory rounds out what students learn from their biology books.

thirty years, Hirsch said, schools have not focused on such basic facts or, at best, have presented them in such a hazy form that students do not remember them. Other people besides Hirsch have noticed this decline in once-common knowledge. Journalist and novelist Benjamin J. Stein described discussions he had with university students in California:

> My particular favorite . . . was the junior at the University of California at Los Angeles who thought that Toronto [Canada] must be in Italy. My second-favorite . . . is the junior at USC [the University of Southern California], a pre-law student, who thought that Washington, D.C. was in Washington State.

The reason why students do not develop a common body of knowledge stems in part from the wide range of classes each school offers. Each school district in the nation, and sometimes each school within a district, has its own set of educational goals. And each school offers a huge range of classes in different subjects—from straight academics like history and science to trade skills like auto shop or carpentry. With so many different class offerings, students rarely find themselves learning the same information.

"Those who graduate from the same school have often studied different subjects," Hirsch said, "and those who graduate from different

"DO US A FAVOR. TRY TO SOUND EDUCATED."

schools have often studied different materials even when their courses have carried the same titles." The result of this overwhelming diversity "is a lack of shared knowledge across and within schools."

A laundry-list approach?

Some education experts oppose Hirsch's theories for a number of reasons. Mostly, they believe that the notion of cultural literacy encourages a shallow, laundry-list approach toward learning. Building up a store of facts might help individuals win board games like "Trivial Pursuit," but it does not mean that they will be better prepared for adult life. Leila Christenbury, a professor at Virginia Commonwealth University, said that teaching this type of "cocktail-party knowledge . . . bears little relation to true education."

Other educators support Hirsch's view, saying

that the primary purpose of American education must be to raise American children to be American adults. This does not mean ignoring or putting down the cultural heritage of the many groups in America or those of the other nations of the world. However, they say, there is a distinct American character and culture, and for the country and its citizens to thrive, this culture must be the main one taught in the public schools.

Hirsch himself has been working on ways to apply his theories to the schools. In 1987 he established the Core Knowledge Foundation of Charlottesville, Virginia, to apply his ideas about cultural literacy. Over the next three years he and a group of other educators developed a program for teachers to use as part of their basic lesson plan. The program was designed to be used during a student's entire school career. Each year's lessons built directly on knowledge the students gained the year before. The program left room for teachers to tailor it to the needs and goals of their own school districts. And it included references to the entire range of America's cultural heritage. For instance, it presented speeches by Abraham Lincoln and by Chief Joseph, leader of the Nez Percé Indian tribe.

Encouraging signs

The Core Knowledge curriculum began its first field test in 1990. The principal of Three Oaks Elementary School in Fort Meyers, Florida, learned about Hirsch's new method of education and allowed the foundation to bring its program to the school. Whether or not the program will be as beneficial as the foundation hopes will not be known for a few years. But it seems to have already had a positive effect. According to an article in the magazine *The Economist*, "the principal . . . reports encouraging signs. Attendance is up, suspensions are down, and the number of students held back has declined." In the meantime, schools in New York, Chicago, Philadelphia, San Antonio, Oklahoma City, and the Mississippi Delta region also have begun using the program.

Innumeracy

The idea behind cultural literacy is that a society can be literate only with the support of a shared core of basic knowledge. Yet some educators have suggested that a society with a poor grasp of how to use numbers is as badly off as one with a large population that cannot read or write. There are many signs that more Americans suffer from numerical illiteracy, or innumeracy, than suffer from language-based illiteracy. One such sign is the U.S. Department of Education and National Science Foundation study showing that American thirteen-year-olds have lower math skills than do teenagers in five other countries. Other studies have shown that American students received less math instruction and homework than do students in Japan or Germany. And fewer college students are majoring in mathematics or in other fields that require an advanced level of math.

John Allen Paulos, a mathematics professor at Temple University, was alarmed at these findings about math in American society. In his 1988 book *Innumeracy: Mathematical Illiteracy and Its Consequences*, Paulos warned that this lack of mathematical understanding could jeopardize the nation's technological future. The world is becoming increasingly dependent on computers and other high-technology equipment. Even today, Paulos said in his book, the nation "depends completely on mathematics and science." A person who is literate—in the sense of knowing how to read and write—can learn how to use almost any

A student learns to use a computer. In today's society, people need more skills than just reading and writing to be truly literate.

of these devices without having to understand the mathematics behind them. But a nation that does not have a grasp of mathematics cannot hope to compete technologically with rival nations that have mastered mathematics.

Big needs, sweeping changes

The explanation of America's large number of innumerate citizens lies in the public's attitude towards math, Paulos said. Mathematics is seen as being useful only for scientists, engineers, and other professionals in number-related fields. And people who are good at math, especially children or teenagers, too often are pegged as "nerds." "What's annoying to me," Paulos said in a magazine interview, "is that while illiterates are ashamed of their inability to read, innumerates often take a kind of pride in their mathematical ignorance. People who would never admit to not knowing anything about Shakespeare . . . will openly boast that they can't balance their checkbooks."

The key to reducing innumeracy is to reform the way math is taught, Paulos said. The standard method of teaching mathematics combines lectures on formulas with in-class drills and homework that require students to simply repeat the lessons taught in class. Teaching math this way, Paulos said, is guaranteed to deaden most people's taste for mathematics. A better method is to show students the ideas behind the formulas and let them figure out for themselves the details of how the formulas work.

Other mathematicians have echoed Paulos's views on why math is such a problem for Americans. Julian Weissglass, a mathematician with the Mathematical Sciences Education Board, a private research and education group, said that math classes focus on "being able to reproduce what someone else has done, rather than thinking for yourself. It disables (students) as thinkers in our society."

Some groups have officially called for changes in the way math classes are run. In 1989 the National Council of Teachers of Mathematics published a list of sweeping changes it felt should be made in the nation's math classes. These changes included replacing teacher lectures and classroom work with group projects and discussions. It also advocated a greater use of computers and calculators for the more mechanical tasks of mathematics, allowing the students to focus on the effects of mathematical formulas. There is too much fear among math teachers that students will become dependent upon calculators to do all math, including simple addition and subtraction, the report said. Also, with these devices so prevalent, or widespread, in the world, it does not make sense not to teach students how best to use them.

Applying math to real life

Organizations, including the Mathematical Sciences Education Board, the American Federation of Teachers, and the National Education Association, came out in support of the suggested changes. "However," an article in the magazine

Students work on math problems on the classroom blackboard. Studies show that students in Japan and Germany outperform American students in math.

Science said, "resistance may be expected from teachers who believe there is no substitute for drillwork and rote memorization to pound facts into young minds."

There are some experimental programs around the nation that use alternative methods to teach math. The *San Jose Mercury News*, a northern California newspaper, described how these classes work.

Small groups of students tackle problems. The students read about the lives of mathematicians and explore how math relates to poetry, art, and music. Independent study is encouraged and projects include describing the aerodynamics of airplanes, deciphering codes, and determining the odds in gambling.

In one such math class at Silver Creek High School in San Jose, students may be grouped to do exercises in probability—for instance, figuring out the chance of rolling a seven with two dice three times in a row. During one exam, the newspaper said, the students had "to figure out which of two telephone companies offered the cheapest service, and then to write a letter describing what they'd learned so far."

This type of teaching method forces the students to take a more active part in learning and applying math skills, rather than simply taking notes while a teacher lectures. And the method seems to work. "I hated math," said one of the Silver Creek math students. "My math classes were boring. But in this class, I started liking it. We work together—we don't do everything alone."

Illiteracy forever?

Many people in the literacy field feel that discussions of innumeracy or cultural literacy are frivolous and take attention away from the widespread lack of general literacy. Yet one of the big

Finding new ways to teach difficult subjects has helped educators in the battle against illiteracy. These students find learning verbal and math skills is more fun using a computer.

questions in the literacy field is, what do people do after they learn how to read? If they do not have the information they need to apply their new literacy skills, then why bother teaching them to read in the first place? Even more important, supporters of an expanded view of literacy argue that by reforming the education system to include cultural and numerical literacy, fewer students in the future will grow up to be illiterate.

However achieved, the need for improved levels of general literacy—skills in reading and writing—is undeniable. But reaching this goal will demand that the nation answer some hard questions. One of the most important of these is, how much can we afford to pay for literacy? Teaching every illiterate teenager and adult in the United States how to read and write will take lots of money. Since the early 1960s the government has spent millions of dollars on various large- and small-scale programs that were supposed to wipe out illiteracy. Private literacy organizations have spent still more money on the problem. Yet these days, according to some experts, one out of three adults is functionally or totally illiterate. We have to ask if we can afford to spend millions of dollars more on further programs that may or may not work. But we also have to ask if we can afford the harm to society if we do not make the effort.

Organizations to Contact

Below are a few of the national literacy organizations in the United States. Other organizations and institutions, including the YMCA, community colleges, and public libraries, may also offer literacy programs.

Barbara Bush Foundation for Family Literacy
1002 Wisconsin Ave. NW
Washington, DC 20007

This organization, named after former First Lady Barbara Bush, helps literacy projects with their start-up costs. It also gives grants to exemplary literacy programs already in operation. The group focuses on projects that provide literacy training for illiterate families as a whole, rather than just for individuals. It also helps volunteer literacy tutors and full-time literacy teachers get training.

Laubach Literacy International
Laubach Literacy Action
PO Box 131
Syracuse, NY 13210
(315) 442-9121

Founded in 1955 by Frank C. Laubach, this organization has provided adult literacy training around the world. Its U.S. program, Laubach Literacy Action, teaches people how to participate in the growth of society as well as how to read, write, listen, and speak effectively and perform basic mathematics. In 1991 Laubach Literacy Action was made up of 105,000 trainers and volunteer tutors, who served more than 150,000 adult students in forty-four states. It also provides tutoring materials for local literacy programs. Its Center for Workforce Education provides a network between businesses and adult education programs.

The Literacy Network, Inc.
7505 Metro Blvd.
Minneapolis, MN 55435

This organization works to build information and communications networks among national, state, and local literacy programs.

Literacy Volunteers of America, Inc. (LVA)
5795 Widewaters Parkway
Syracuse, NY 13214
(315) 445-8000

This national organization provides free tutoring through a network of 450 community programs in forty-five states. LVA's programs cover both basic literacy skills and English as a second language. Adults and teenagers meet with their tutors in one-on-one sessions or small groups. Founded in 1962, the program currently has more than 125,000 volunteer tutors and students.

Reading Is Fundamental, Inc. (RIF)
600 Maryland Ave. SW, Suite 500
Washington, DC 20024
(202) 287-3220

A children's literacy organization founded in 1966, RIF currently serves about three million young people a year. Its programs focus on making reading an enjoyable experience. The organization gives books to students in grades five through twelve and urges families and communities to take part in reading activities. RIF also helps middle school and high school students conduct reading programs for younger children.

Women of the Evangelical Lutheran Church in America (ELCA)
8765 West Higgins Road
Chicago, IL 60631
(800) 638-3522

This church-based group was formed in 1988 when three Lutheran church women's groups merged. One of those groups was the Lutheran Church Women, which had sponsored what was the nation's largest church-based literacy project. Currently, the Women of the ELCA works mainly to educate the public about the problems facing illiterate Americans. It does, however, publish some literacy instruction materials.

Suggestions for Further Reading

Leila Christenbury, "Cultural Literacy: A Terrible Idea Whose Time Has Come," *English Journal*, January 1989.

Dan Chu, "An Eminent Math Professor Says 'Innumeracy' Rivals Illiteracy as a Cause for Concern in America," *People Weekly*, May 29, 1989.

The Economist, "Common Knowledge," June 20, 1992.

Marie Costa, *Adult Literacy/Illiteracy in the United States: A Handbook for Reference and Research*. Santa Barbara, CA: ABC-Clio, 1988.

David Harman, *Illiteracy: A National Dilemma*. New York: Cambridge Book Company, 1987.

E. D. Hirsch, *Cultural Literacy: What Every American Needs to Know*. Boston: Houghton Mifflin, 1987.

Shoshana Daniel Kerewsky, "Playing with Cultural Literacy," *English Journal*, January 1989.

Jonathan Kozol, *Illiterate America*. Garden City, NY: Anchor Press/Doubleday, 1985.

John Allen Paulos, *Innumeracy: Mathematical Illiteracy and Its Consequences*. New York: Hill and Wang, 1988.

Psychology Today, "Making the Best of It: The Trials and Triumphs of Being Learning Disabled," January 1986.

Jeffrey L. Salter and Charles A. Salter, *Literacy and the Library*. Englewood, CO: Libraries Unlimited, 1991.

Jonathan Weisman, "The Education Smokescreen," *Phi Delta Kappan*, May 1992.

Works Consulted

Elaine Adams, "Illiteracy: A Waste of Good Minds," *Kansas City* (Missouri) *Star*, September 8, 1991.

Louise Applebome, "Illiteracy in America: An Emotional Appeal from 7 Adults and Their Reading Tutors," *Dallas Morning News*, November 11, 1990.

Michael Bernick, "Illiteracy and Inner-City Unemployment," *Phi Delta Kappan*, January 1986.

Better Homes and Gardens, "Is Your Child Being Tracked for Failure?" October 1988.

H. S. Bhola, *Campaigning for Literacy*. Paris: United Nations Educational, Scientific, and Cultural Organization, 1984.

A. Phillips Brooks, "Literacy Program Hopes to Break Cycle of Crime," *Austin* (Texas) *American-Statesman*, November 24, 1990.

Beverly H. Butterworth, "Literacy Programs Make Their Mark," *The* (Portland) *Oregonian*, September 7, 1988.

Marie Carbo, "Deprogramming Reading Failure: Giving Unequal Learners an Equal Chance," *Phi Delta Kappan*, November 1987.

Jeanne S. Chall et al., "Adult Literacy: New and Enduring Problems," *Phi Delta Kappan*, November 1987.

Forrest P. Chisman and Associates, *Leadership for Literacy*. San Francisco: Jossey-Bass, 1990.

Glennda Chui, "Calculated Risks," *San Jose* (California) *Mercury News*, February 5, 1991.

Muriel Cohen, "State Literacy Effort Found Aiding Less Than 5% of Needy," *Boston Globe*, March 22, 1990.

(Columbia, South Carolina) *State*, "The Facts and Fiction About U.S. Illiteracy," September 4, 1988.

Michael D'Antonio, "Learning Styles" and "When an IQ Test is Wrong," (Long Island, New York) *Newsday*, August 23, 1988.

Brad Darrach and Dianna Waggoner, "A Success as a Teacher and Builder, John Corcoran Had a Humiliating Secret: He Couldn't Read or Write," *People Weekly*, December 5, 1988.

Tracie Dungan, "Definition of Literacy Put Under Pressure by Information Age," (Little Rock) *Arkansas Democrat*, September 8, 1991.

David Elliot, "Program Combats Illiteracy," *Austin* (Texas) *American-Statesman*, February 4, 1991.

Howard Fields, "Barbara Bush Foundation for Family Literacy Launched at White House," *Publishers Weekly*, March 24, 1989.

Howard Fields, "Literacy Bill Progresses with Senate's Okay," *Publishers Weekly*, July 19, 1991.

Howard Fields, "$1.1 Billion Literacy Spending Bill Becomes Law," *Publishers Weekly*, August 16, 1991.

Bill Goodling, "Literacy Education Gives Second Chance to Many Who Need It," (Washington, D.C.) *Roll Call*, March 18, 1991.

Christine Gorman, "The Literacy Gap," *Time*, December 19, 1988.

Rosemary Harty, "The Faces of Illiteracy," (Dayton, Ohio) *Daily News/Journal Herald*, December 2, 1990.

Steve Harvey, "Drawing Dropouts Back to School," (Atlanta) *Journal*, December 24, 1990.

Sam Heys, "60 Million Americans Pay Price Daily for Illiteracy," (Atlanta) *Journal*, August 25, 1986.

Miriam Horn, "The Burgeoning Educational Underclass," *U.S. News & World Report*, May 18, 1987.

Carman St. John Hunter with David Harman, *Adult Illiteracy in the United States: A Report to the Ford Foundation*. New York: McGraw-Hill, 1979.

Jan Jaben, "Illiteracy: Who Pays When Johnny Can't Read?" *Folio: The Magazine for Magazine Management*, April 1989.

Russel Kleinbach, "Nicaraguan Literacy Campaign: Its Democratic Essence," *Monthly Review*, July/August 1985.

Jonathan Kozol, *Prisoners of Silence: Breaking the Bonds of Adult Illiteracy in the United States*. New York: Continuum, 1980.

Los Angeles Times, "Fewer Firms Testing Employee Literacy," August 12, 1992.

Leonard Lund and E. Patrick McGuire, *Literacy in the Work Force*. New York: The Conference Board, 1990.

Gary E. McCuen, *Illiteracy in America*. Hudson, WI: Gary E. McCuen Publications, 1988.

Hattie McGowan, "Never Too Late: A Literacy Tutor's Story," *Wilson Library Bulletin*, February 1990.

Robert McNergney and Martin Haberman, "Retention Holds Kids Back," *NEA Today*, November 1989.

Deanna B. Marcum and Elizabeth W. Stone, "Illiteracy: The Library Legacy," *American Libraries*, March 1991.

Guy Maxtone-Graham, "Lacking Tutors, Adult Illiterates Pull Together," *Los Angeles Times*, September 10, 1988.

Stanley Meisler, "Reading the Signs of Crisis," *Los Angeles Times*, May 11, 1990.

Elizabeth Mullener, "Literacy Spells Independence," (New Orleans) *Times-Picayune*, December 18, 1990.

Elizabeth Mullener, "N.O. Gets Literacy Grant," (New Orleans) *Times-Picayune*, June 8, 1992.

Frankie Pelzman, "BBF [Barbara Bush Foundation] Literacy Grants," *Wilson Library Bulletin*, February 1992.

Barbara Prete, "Business Defines Its Role," *Publishers Weekly*, May 26, 1989.

Prevention, "When Reading Isn't Fundamental," September 1991.

Deana Priest, "Employees Upgrade Basic Work Skills," *The Washington Post*, July 17, 1992.

Shelley Quezada, "Strengthening the Library Network for Literacy," *Wilson Library Bulletin*, February 1990.

James C. Raymond, ed., *Literacy as a Human Problem*. Birmingham: University of Alabama Press, 1982.

Mary Ann Roser, "Toyota to Give $2 Million to Literacy Program," *Lexington* (Kentucky) *Herald-Leader*, January 31, 1991.

Ron Russell, "Successful 'Learn to Read' Campaign Will Be Continued," *Detroit News*, September 8, 1986.

Steven Schulman, "Facing the Invisible Handicap," *Psychology Today*, February 1986.

Science, "Big Changes Urged for Precollege Math," March 1989.

Gary Smith, "The Man Who Couldn't Read," *Esquire*, August 1990.

Mary Lee Smith and Lorrie A. Shepard, "What Doesn't Work: Explaining Policies of Retention in the Early Grades," *Phi Delta Kappan*, October 1987.

Lucia Solorzano and Andrea Atkins, "Will Staying Back Help or Hurt?" *Ladies' Home Journal*, September 1990.

George Steiner, "Little-Read Schoolhouse," *The New Yorker*, June 1, 1987.

Joan C. Szabo, "Boosting Workers' Basic Skills," *Nation's Business*, January 1992.

Denise Thornton, "Mathematician: Innumeracy Adds Up to Problem," *South Bend* (Indiana) *Tribune*, January 30, 1991.

Sheila Tobias, "Tracked to Fail," *Psychology Today*, September 1989.

UN Chronicle, "Launching the Possible Dream," March 1990.

Judith M. Warner, "Illiteracy May Affect Businesses More than Most Bosses Realize," (Camp Hill, Pennsylvania) *Central Penn Business Journal*, September 1, 1991.

Index

About the Author

Free-lance writer Sean M. Grady received a bachelor of arts degree in print journalism from the University of Southern California in 1988. While in college he worked for the entertainment section of the *Los Angeles Times* as a reporting intern; for *California* magazine as a research intern; and for the City News Service of Los Angeles, a local news wire, as a general assignment reporter. During the two years after his graduation, Grady specialized in business reporting and worked as business editor of the *Olympian*, a daily newspaper in Olympia, Washington. Grady currently lives in Sparks, Nevada.

Picture Credits